I0786532

SELF-DISCIPLINE MADE EASY

Achieve your goals, learn how self-control works and beat procrastination

By Joshua Moore and Basil Foster

FREE DOWNLOAD

INSIGHTFUL GROWTH STRATEGIES FOR YOUR PERSONAL AND PROFESSIONAL SUCCESS!

amazonkindle   nook   kobo   iBooks

Windows   android   BlackBerry

Sign up here to get a free copy of The Growth Mindset book and more:

www.frenchnumber.net/growth

Table of contents

CHAPTER 1. INTRO

I have a confession to make.

The last thing I want to do right now is write.

You read that correctly. I would rather be outside going for a hike in the woods or taking a long walk in my neighborhood.

Heck, I'd rather be washing the dishes right now rather than sitting at a keyboard stringing words together.

I understand the irony too. Here I am writing a book about self-discipline and how to develop more of it, yet as I write this my self-discipline is at an all-time low.

However, understand this too. I am writing when I don't want to write. That means something. It is taking discipline to sit down and type out words onto a computer screen when I would rather do something else.

This book will lay out in detail how I am able to accomplish the things I accomplish on a regular basis. I have spoken with and studied multiple experts in the field and can say with great assuredness that this stuff works.

I am very excited to share them with you and believe it will have a profound impact on your life if you are able to implement the strategies I will lay out.

From starting small to positive imaging the techniques and tactics I endorse will be effective and the more you use them the bigger role in your life they will play.

The idea of self-discipline is just the first step. Too many people try to do it all at once and fail miserably. The gym right after people set New Year's resolutions and two weeks later is littered with discarded ambitions of developing better habits. The simple truth is you need to start small and gain micro victories which will lead to greater ones down the road.

Rome was not built in a day, they say. However, as James Clear points out, they were laying the bricks every hour. In other words, do not let the big picture of creating more self-discipline in your life be overshadowed by the small tasks that need to be accomplished every day.

Your routines and habits play such a big role in your development, from just feeling better about yourself to landing the job or starting the business of your dreams. With good habit and self-discipline in place the world can truly be your oyster.

People are always looking for the magic bullet. What they do not realize is the magic bullet is right is inside of them. By being able to harness the power of your mind and put it to work on the goals you want to accomplish, you truly can achieve anything you set your mind to.

Here's something else you can expect once you establish these new habits and discipline into your life. You will be able to see through a lot of marketing and hype designed to 'show' you how to be more productive when in reality all it is interested in is taking your money.

What do I mean by that?

Well, there are many guru's and consultants out there making a living from telling you to be more productive and if you just listen to them and implement their system then all of your problems will be solved.

You and I both know this is probably not going to happen. Something occurs when we subject ourselves to an 'expert'. We tend to shut off the analytical part of our brain and accept what they say as gospel. Here's the thing. In order to progress we need to be able to figure things out for ourselves and use what works for us. Self-discipline is something that once it is developed and strengthened will allow us to carve our own path.

That may sound counter-intuitive coming from me. After all, I'm writing a book about self-discipline. How am I any different from what everyone else is saying out there?

It's a fair question. Here's my answer. I am looking to give you the tools to help you succeed with this book realizing you will have what you need going forward to blaze your own trail.

This may sound like a subtle difference but I assure you it is profound. My goal is for you to be able to succeed on your own. Use this book to refer back to from time to time but trust what I tell you in this introduction, you have what it takes to develop powerful habits and the self-discipline to accomplish the goals of your dreams.

CHAPTER 2. Foundational Habits

As we begin our journey into self-discipline there are fundamentals that we should focus on first before we tackle the big ones, such as better relationships or a career change, or starting a business.

All of these things require tremendous self-discipline and willpower, at least in the beginning. If you were to jump into these things without having a solid foundation in place, you may find yourself discouraged and in over your head before you know it.

What are some good habits to develop first?

If you want a good starting place go with sleep, nutrition, exercise and mindfulness. These can form the foundation for you to springboard into other areas of your life and you will enter those areas with renewed confidence because you have accomplished these foundational habits of self-discipline first.

Let's start with sleep. You should be aiming for 7

to 8 hours per night, this means you may have to go to bed earlier but that is what you are aiming for the ability to wake up feeling refreshed and ready to tackle your day. Perhaps you have gotten into the habit of watching TV late at night, we now live at a time when you can record the shows or they are available on other streaming services that will give you the ability to watch them whenever your schedule allows. So use the weekend instead of staying up past 10 during the week when you should be laying down in bed. We are a sleep starved nation/world and we need more than we think. Many people think they can get by on 4 to 5 hours a night and still feel productive. I am here to tell you that is false. There are very few people in the world that only need four hours of sleep and I can almost guarantee you are not one of them. The problem is you have developed the habit of only sleeping four hours a night so you really do not know any different and you think you feel okay but you don't you are and I assure you less productive and less able to focus on complex tasks when you are sleep deprived.

Make setting up a new bedtime routine your first habit. Let that become a ritual for you.

Number one. Keep your bedroom dark and try to avoid reading electronic devices when you are in your room. The bedroom should be for two things in two things only sex and sleep. Electronic devices emit blue light which can wreck havoc on the circadian rhythm, causing you to not even realize that your sleep cycle has been compromised.

Number two. Keep it cool fans help a lot and keeping the air conditioning between 70 75° can help tremendously, especially augmented with a fan.

Number three. you want to quiet. Use earplugs or have the fan which is you are using to call yourself also use that as a white noise generator. If you have noisy neighbors. This can help a great deal.

Number four. Do not engage in strenuous exercise within three hours or so bedtime. Your body does not realize, nor can it tell the difference between you running at the gym on the treadmill and that you ran from saber tooth tiger to avoid being eaten. It needs time to calm down exercise. Of course, earlier in the day is outstanding and wonderful for your health, as well as improving your sleep, but not right before bed.

Number five. Avoid caffeine after 2 PM. A lot of people think having caffeine does not affect them and they are possibly right in that there is some tolerance buildup to it over time. However, in general, it is better to just stay away from caffeinated drinks five or six hours before you go to bed, if not longer.

And of course...

Number six. Don't smoke. This in addition to every other health issue that it causes can be very detrimental to your sleep.

How to optimize your sleep

What this means is how long do you really need to sleep, everyone within a range needs between 6 1/2 to 8 hours sleep a night.

You do not know what your quotient is until you try it.

Go to bed at your normal time and then do not set an alarm to wake up. Simply wake up and see what time you wait you get up if you wake up feeling refreshed and ready to tackle your day. That is your number. If it was, for example, seven hours, always shoot for seven hours every night. It will be part of this routine that you're developing and you were going to be incredibly productive and your self-discipline is going to shoot through the roof because with rest comes greater will power.

Center yourself before bed. Listen to calming

music, don't watch extremely violent or action-packed movies before bed. Focus on something quiet and restful so that your body eases into sleep at night and you will feel the benefits of it in the morning.

Another important foundation that you need to look at is your nutrition. Use this as an opportunity to develop self-discipline. For example, when you do your shopping pick healthy foods. Make a list before you go in there and hold yourself to that list to find the foods that are going to be the most beneficial for you and your body.

Something else I recommend is trying intermittent fasting. Intermittent fasting is essentially a modified form of going without food for an extended period of time. There are several benefits to this that I think you will find very interesting.

Number one, it cuts down on the amount of calories you taken because you are cutting yourself down from eating over a 12 -14 hour period. Breakfast in the morning lunch in the afternoon, dinner in the evening so we would say that's probably a 12 hour window of eating. All you do is simply cut that window of eating down to eight hours.

For example, eat your first meal at noon and then you will eat your last meal at say 8 PM. By cutting down the feeding time, you will automatically cut down your calories. If you are eating similar foods, you will also find that eventually your body adjusts to this new feeding time and you won't even feel hungry until the appointed time, say noon, in this case.

The other option is to try whatever diet works for you. I believe intermittent fasting is something that a lot of people can benefit from. There are other studies that are showing intermittent fasting to be beneficial for the prevention of heart disease as well as not developing diabetes. Of course, your food choices will play into this. You cannot undertake intermittent fasting and then eat whatever you want. You need to have some type of mindfulness about the food choices you are making.

However, if you are making good food choices and you employ intermittent fasting, I believe you can see increased benefits versus a more traditional eating time.

The thinking about this and this gets a little bit scientific, (but not too much) is your body thinks it is still in a hunter gatherer type environment so there were times when people would go out to hunt and they would not eat until they found food so the concept of having a breakfast lunch and dinner to our forefathers and those that came before us is probably foreign.

They were probably eating only once a day. We in modern civilization are very spoiled in that we get to eat pretty much whatever we want whenever we want with ever-increasing abundance by putting this constraint on yourself.

You are able to see the benefits of calorie restriction as well as warding off other disease states caused by eating too much, such as diabetes. Another thing you can do is set the times you have sweets or treats to one day per week and then try to keep it to one meal per week.

This is another way of developing self-discipline in your life and will help you cut down on your consumption of foods that are not as good for you.

I have found that increasing the healthy fats in the diet significantly cuts down on the craving people have for carbohydrates, and especially the more sugary and refined carbohydrates.

Another thing you will want to do is keep alcohol consumption to a minimum. Do not drink within several hours of going to bed. This disrupts your sleep-wake cycle. It has been shown that alcohol prevents you from going into the REM or rapid eye movement sleep where the rejuvenation and true healing that sleep provides takes place. At the very least keep it to a minimum.

Exercise.

If they could bottle exercise, it would be marketed as a miracle cure and the answer to many of life's ills.

It would also be touted as helping you avoid most of the chronic diseases many of us face later in life such as diabetes and heart disease as well as cancer.

Regular exercise is one of those foundations, you should be working to develop before you do anything else. By having this in place along with solid nutrition, solid sleep, you are setting yourself up for great success.

Start slow, take the stairs instead of the elevator when you go to work. Have your gym clothes laid out and ready to go the night before so that when you get up you know you are going to work out as soon as you walk out the door. Sleep in your gym clothes. It's the same idea - you wake up ready to go. All you have to do is put on your shoes and go outside make it part of your routine.

Eventually it will become second nature and the benefits you get from exercise along with that endorphin rush you get from participating in sweating and pushing yourself. It's like a built-in therapy session, you get every time you work out. Find what interests you. It may not be going to the gym. It may be working in your garden. It may be taking long walks supplemented with body weight exercises. There are so many ways that you can go about this. It is up to you to find what works for you.

You just need to move.

Meditation and mindfulness

Regular meditation has been shown to increase a person's ability to focus and endure far longer than someone who does not practice in this on a regular basis.

Why and what does it entail? Simply sitting still in trying to clear mind? Well yes and no. It isn't that easy. You will find yourself with what Buddhist monks call monkey brain where your mind wants to endlessly chatter and focus on something and we were trying to quiet it. It seems like it will go into overdrive and all of a sudden you can't get your mind off of needless tasks that normally would not be on your mind. They suddenly become first and foremost the most important things in the world, such as doing the laundry.

That is okay. This is part of the natural process.

We live in an environment, especially with social media and constant Internet access to always be on and always be searching for new information.

These mindfulness techniques that you develop over time will help you to quiet that to where you will not need to have constant stimulation. This is the goal where you don't feel that you have to have that constant stimulation. Take it easy on yourself and understand that it takes time and eventually things will begin to quiet. Allow those thoughts to flow through like on a stream and they just float on by. Don't judge them, just see them for what they are and then they begin to quiet on their own. You will get better at this with practice.

That's almost a contradictory term but you do improve your ability to quiet your mind, even though it is not a competition. The more discipline you can impose into your life will result from consistent meditation. Why is that? It's because now you are in control of your thoughts. You are now able to direct where you're going to put your energy and you will not be like a leaf blowing in the wind, trying to stay upright, you will simply be and then you can find what you need to focus on and you can put your energy there with a singular focus which will be talking about a lot in this book. There are many resources out there to develop a meditation habit. My recommendation is the practicing mind by Thomas Sterner. In his book he details anecdotes from his life as well as people that he's worked with and shown that by quieting the mind and by being in control of one's thoughts, the ability to get things done is almost exponential in its power.

These four fundamental habits I believe need to be looked at first before you start looking at individual habits and aspects of self-discipline that you want to develop these four things put in place will help give you that springboard to success in other areas and if you take it in that line of thinking.

You will see huge benefits by just mastering them first. Everything else will follow.

Chapter 3. The 'Just Do Something' Principle

Just do something already.

Oftentimes we as human beings live inside of our own heads and fail to get out of them.

I think you know what I mean here you have this big idea for a business you want to start or a book you want to write or someone you want to ask out or something along those lines.

However, before you even begin you have already talked yourself out of it and given yourself a thousand and one reasons why it won't work before it even starts.

Sure, you would love to have that business, you would love to have that book written. Go on that date with that special someone.

However, there are just too many things and it just seems so daunting that you cannot see yourself finishing, heck you can't even see yourself starting for that matter.

Here is the deal, you need to start somewhere.

It may not be much but it is a start. Do something that furthers that goal along.

So instead of looking at this as a huge project that is going to take up all of your time and resources, instead look at it as a series of small steps.

In his excellent book the Checklist Manifesto, Atul Gawande explains how giant skyscrapers are created. You would think it would be completely and utterly overwhelming to even conceive taking on a task such as that. However, when it is broken down into its component parts, you see that it is simply a series of steps and checklists that need to be followed.

So why is your career or dream or ambition any different? Why is it you cannot fathom a better life for yourself?

It can be incredibly paralyzing if you take this large view of the entire project or dream you have. The fact of the matter is, you are correct, it is too big to handle all at once and all by yourself.

Here's what you do instead of looking at the entire project and becoming overwhelmed...take it one step at a time.

For example, let's say you want to write a book. You have been dreaming about this for years. However, now is the time, so you set aside an hour and decide you are going to tackle it. But you sit down at your desk and you do not even know where to begin. You are suffering from what is known as analysis paralysis. You do not need to suffer from this. Simply write a sentence. Be easy on yourself. Tell yourself, that's all I need to do today is write one sentence. If I get that one sentence out, then I will be done for the day and I can go and enjoy my time with my family and loved ones. Sometimes that is all the time we have.

Give yourself permission to start small.

Give yourself permission to not finish in one sitting.

When you do this you will see that your inhibitions and the procrastination that has been holding you back all along will begin to disappear.

You will suddenly find yourself writing far more than one sentence. You will have written a paragraph before you know it. This is a great feeling and will give you the confidence to keep going.

Tell yourself you are going to do this every day.

You are just going to write one sentence per day.

If you do this I can guarantee you will finish what you start. Nothing saps our confidence more than not completing projects we set out to complete.

However, if you give yourself permission to not be perfect, you are more than likely going to finish your book. Will it be a masterpiece? Probably not. But that is okay, it doesn't matter. The fact of the matter is you finished and that something to be proud of. That is something that is going to build momentum in your life. It is going to put you in the right direction of becoming a better writer in this particular instance.

It can apply to other things as well. Let's say you are interested in becoming a business owner. There are many resources out there, and a lot of them are very good. You read through them and make a plan of action.

Here is what happens though, you become paralyzed by what steps to take next. Perhaps you do not know the field as well, as you thought you did, for you are someone who is very good at what they do, but may not understand the business side of things such as invoicing, business taxes, business, law, etc. Do not let that stop you, all it means is you need to get more education in the areas you are a little weak in and there is nothing wrong with that and it does not mean that you can't start.

Let let's say for example you want to start a web design business. You have the experience, the connections, and the expertise. Those are good things, but perhaps you have not been has exposed to the things I mentioned earlier, such as tax law, etc. It is worth making a call to an accountant or lawyer that specializes in this type of set up and get some advice. They will usually give you a free consultation to begin with as a courtesy. If you do not have money to afford one up front just get some advice to begin so you are starting in the correct direction. Get some clients and save up and then hire them later. Ask a lot of questions.

Another option you can do is very thorough research online. There will be sometimes where you will need an attorney's advice but for most things, you should be able to figure out what you need to do and just use common sense. Obviously this isn't a business book so don't construe that as advice. Have a bias towards action.

My point in all this is. Do not let fear of the unknown stop. You simply move forward. Do one thing a day in your business. It could be as simple as opening your website and making putting up the graphics that you need or a portfolio samples or something that shows you are capable and willing to help another business out.

You have taken each step and broken it down into its component parts, to show yourself that you can do it.

Do one thing a day.

If you do this you will be up and running in no time. The alternative is you keep talking yourself out of moving forward because your mind will come up with all sorts of excuses as to why this cannot happen.

Why is that? It's because the brain loves the known. It craves safety and security. It will do everything to talk you out of moving forward.

My advice just do something. Do something that will propel the business forward that day. Do something that will make you take action and override your tendency to hesitate.

One step leads to two which leads to three and so on.

Make this a part of your self-discipline mastery. It will pay off.

CHAPTER 4. Fight Your Dopamine Addiction

Dopamine is a neurotransmitter synthesized in the brain and is responsible for many roles both in the brain and the body.

In the brain - It plays a major role in motivation and is an integral part of the reward and motivation behavior cycle. It is also responsible for motor movement control, memory, attention, mood, cognition, and sleep. It is also known as the main chemical associated with motivation and desire. This function of the cells responsible for dopamine production leads to different disease states, including Parkinson's disease, possibly an association with ADHD, attention deficit hyperactivity disorder and schizophrenia. In other words, is a very important neurotransmitter.

For our purposes, let's look at its function in the nervous system where it plays a major role in executive function, motor control, motivation, arousal, reinforcement and reward (Wikipedia).

Dopamine is released to reinforce pleasurable activities. It is related to our level of ambition, addiction, sex drive and desire. It is how habits are formed by anticipating a reward for an action. Let's say for example you go to the gym and work out and you feel amazing. Eventually, you become addicted to the feeling you get, post-workout and do everything you can to make sure you feel that endorphin rush.

Or, say, are less positive note, you begin shooting heroin into your veins. The pleasure you feel from that high will you receive will override other more pressing matters such as the fact that you become hopelessly addicted to something that is very difficult to quit and could in a very real sense kill you as well as your relationships, self-esteem, and everything else associated with living a full life.

It does not discriminate, dopamine is simply a process that once employed, seeks pleasure whether the activity is healthy or not.

Much of social media along with everything else of the Internet is designed to distract us from our daily lives.

It is been admitted by social media giant Facebook that the network was founded not to unite us but to distract us. (Simon Park – the Guardian, March 4, 2018)

Here is what is happening in our modern world. The social media juggernaut and everything else is marketing nonstop to you, trying everything in their power to get your attention. Games are designed to reward you and distract you that you play endlessly while being subtly advertised to the entire time.

Do you ever wonder where the feed is endless and Facebook and twitter? That isn't an accident, it is designed to make you continually scroll through it. Irregularly timed rewards, a technique taken from slot machine designers also keeps us glued to our phones. They have shown that when gamblers who felt they were aided by luck are more likely to stick around and continue gambling than if the reward was more predictable. This causes an increase in dopamine. We are always looking for something new in our feeds, giving us a little pang of dopamine each time we are quote "rewarded" with a new update.

This is truly amazing if you stop and think about it. It is almost as if it was from a cheesy movie from the 1960s with the mad scientists working to brainwash the masses into what they want to do. Alas, it is the reality of today that we give it willingly because it feels so good.

At least in the short run, it does. Most people feel a sense of emptiness and can't quite put their finger on what is wrong, but know something is off when they are spending too much time on social media.

All of this attention grabbing is hijacking our brain's ability to make decisions and to complete tasks because we are so addicted to our phones and the dopamine rush we get from playing games and scrolling through social media sites.

It makes willpower a moot point.

So what can we do about it?

Face it, you have been desensitized to dopamine. It is one of the reasons you cannot commit to anything you feel like you used to be able to. It is not your imagination. The fact of the matter is to recognize that it is happening in the first place.

Are you opening a tab for social media site, not realizing that you already have one open? Mark Manson talks about this on his blog, having Facebook open them without even thinking about it, opening another tab and typing in Facebook.

Are you incessantly checking email? If you are, don't beat yourself up too much about it. Forces have been conspiring against you for a long time and are very good at getting your attention.

Here's what you do.

1.   Go on a social media diet. Don't do it all at once, of course. That would be setting yourself up for failure, not success, and would only serve to frustrate you. Begin with not checking your email until a set time, say 10 AM if you get to work at eight and leave the mornings free to pursue your work.

2.   Cut out porn. Nothing, and I mean nothing, hijacks the brain easier or more completely than pornography. No matter what your moral stance is on it, from a dopamine standpoint it is a problem. Porn is probably the most effective at taking over and becoming an obsession. It cuts to the core of who we are and what we are as human beings and our need for sex and to procreate. It does not matter if you want kids or not, the drive for sex is nearly universal. By becoming dependent on porn can lead to a whole host of other issues such as erectile dysfunction in men as well as having trouble forming healthy relationships with another person. This is something I say you should leave sooner rather than later. It will not be easy

but is very worth it. Once you have given yourself some time away from it, it will begin to lose its luster to you and you will be more open to healthy relationships.

3.   Stop videogames. Again, this is not a moral stance about violence, etc. in videogames. It is simply that, like porn, it can be overwhelming to the dopamine reward system in our brains. It does this by giving us a sense of accomplishment and the reward system in place is immediate and irregular, making it highly addictive. Replace games with reading a good nonfiction book when you want to do something else.

4.   Cut out or limit junk food. Another way to hijack the dopamine rewards is to continually overload it with sugar and processed food designed to taste amazing. One way to accomplish this is by limiting your junk food consumption to one day per week, say on a Saturday. You might as well throw alcohol consumption into this mix as well because in addition to being highly addictive, it leads to bad decisions and whole host of health problems.

5.   Limit Netflix, YouTube, Amazon, Digital, and all sorts of digital entertainment. All of these have an almost endless supply of entertainment such as we have never seen before. It is possible to have a new way to watch or a new episode to watch every day because by the time you're done with one show they've produced and published new series or episode, etc. Heady times for sure,

but also very capable of robbing you of all of your time. Use these shows as rewards for accomplishing real work and only in short time intervals.

6.   Your phone. Yes I know it is almost heresy to say leave it behind, and there are so many good so many things we can say to justify having with us at all times, but the reality is this, you really don't need to have it with you as much as you think. I have a client who works in a prison. He needs to leave his phone in his car while he's at work. He reported feeling better about not having it seemingly attached to his hand at all times. Once the initial shock of not having it passed. He said he is less apt to use it and he is found other things to take its place, such as reading physical books. Look for ways to minimize using. If you're going to be somewhere where you don't really need it, lock it in your car. I can honestly tell you it's not going anywhere and that call that you are expecting can always call you back.

All of these dopamine robbers will scream and cry for your attention and like spoiled children, they will be shocked and insulted that you are not spending as much time with them. That's okay, by being aware of it you will be in the driver's seat of developing self-discipline and will get these under control. These attention robbers can be controlled and once you do you will see your discipline get stronger and stronger.

CHAPTER 5. WOOP there it is

No, I'm not talking about the popular song from the 1990's. What I am referring to is a scientifically proven way to attain your goals in a manner that embraces all aspects of your personality as well as utilizing aspects of your conscious and subconscious in ways you have probably never thought worked together.

Before we get into WOOP however I want to explain the science behind it.

The concept of mental reframing or cognitive reframing is the process of placing something in a new frame. Our minds work overtime to figure things out and work through both real and imagined dangers it faces on a daily even minute by minute basis.

Reframing involves the process of identifying and replacing negative thoughts with positive ones.

Mental reframing is often used by therapists to help their patients get over and improve negative thought patterns and replace them with more positive or at least constructive ones.

Reframing improves one's mental outlook leading to a better attitude, behaviors, and goal attainment.

Like a muscle the brain will strengthen in areas and atrophy in others depending on the circumstances.

For example, the hippocampus in taxicab drivers in New York City is more developed and physically bigger than that of an average person. The drivers are able to navigate the complex streets and directions with ease because of this.

It can work in other ways as well however. If you are continually showering yourself with negative self-talk then that area of your brain will be strengthened leading a downward spiral of negativity with the result being a negative outlook that can be very difficult to overcome.

Framing has to do with how you view yourself in the world along with your circumstances and beliefs. It is how you assign meaning to situations that present themselves to you. Think of it as the lens we use to view the world.

Depending on your outlook they can be either incredibly helpful by making you see unlimited possibilities in a given situation or harmful because you limit yourself to only a few maybe not so great choices.

Let's take for example a work related project.

If you see yourself as disorganized and lacking in time management, yet you have to get this project done in a timely manner or you risk losing your job.

Any change you make begins with your thoughts.

How you frame your thoughts will enable you to either prosper or fail. It really depends on how you approach it.

In the excellent book 'The Slight Edge', the author Jeff Olson lays out the case that self-help books and diets do not work not for a lack of information. If that were the case we would all have healthy, successful, and fulfilling lives. There has never been more information out there than there is today on how to get ahead, start a business from scratch, to meeting the wife or husband of your dreams. The simple fact of the matter is this, if you do not apply what you learn, then all of the information in the world will not help you attain anything. If your attitude is not lined up correctly with your beliefs then you are going to go through life with very frustrated and wonder why nothing seems to go your way.

Have you noticed that when you begin a diet how easy it is? Effortless even. You are motivated to see it through. But what happens? You lose motivation and soon you are right back where you started.

Enter WOOP.

It stands for Wish, Outcome, Obstacle, Plan.

So, lets stay with our diet example.

You want to lose ten pounds and can see yourself fitting into that pair of jeans you purchased a few years ago but haven't been able to wear in a while.

That's your wish.

Now, imagine how good you are going to look when you put them on. Don't worry, no one is reading your mind. That is your outcome, feeling and looking good in those jeans.

But, you realize that the weekend is coming up and you always go out with friends and maybe drink and eat a little more than usual. This is your obstacle.

So you decide to eat something healthy before you go out that night so you don't eat as much when you are with your friends and you prepare a healthy meal for the next day. You also volunteer to be the designated driver for your friends so you don't have to call a taxi or Uber. This is your plan.

See, most people would like to lose the weight but they don't plan for the inevitable obstacles that pop up. By systematizing your approach and anticipating challenges you now stand a better chance of succeeding.

Try it with anything. It can range from studying for tests to starting a business. In fact, businesses do this all the time with what is called a SWOT analysis which stands for Strengths, Weaknesses, Opportunities, and Threats.

By applying it to habit formation you will stand a better chance of developing better self-discipline.

Chapter 6. Temptation Bundling

What is it?

A term coined by Wharton School of Business professor Catherine Milkman. She holds a joint PhD in computer science and business, however, her passion is behavioral economics, more specifically how it can be applied to people's everyday lives.

Coming home from work in the evening she found she was too tired to go to the gym. Instead she would have rather read or binge watched TV shows on Netflix or Amazon.

One day she discovered the method we are going to explore in this chapter, all because she wanted to read her book, The Hunger Games. She was hit with a sudden burst of inspiration. What if she could only read her book only when she was at the gym?

By imposing this rule upon herself. It would force her to go to the gym to do something she enjoyed

(Freakonomics radio- When Willpower Isn't Enough).

She is quoted as saying, "I struggle at the end of a long day to get myself to the gym. Even though I know that I should go. And at the end of a long day, I also struggle with the desire to watch my favorite TV shows, instead of getting work done. And so I actually realized that those two temptations, those two struggles, I faced, could be combined to solve both problems."

Her strategy worked. She was in the gym more and look forward to it because she was then able to combine something she enjoyed, such as reading or watching her shows with something that would otherwise be easy to put off.

Temptation bundling is the tying together of two activities, one you like or enjoy doing tied to one you are not as excited about doing and will avoid doing.

Or another way of putting it, according to Brian flux and a guide to temptation bundling is to tie a highly enjoyable low beneficial activity with a less enjoyable, but highly beneficial one.

She listed other examples, such as getting a

pedicure while catching up on overdue emails or listening to your favorite music only while you do housework.

You can extend relationships to such as eating at a restaurant where you love to eat the hamburgers but only with a difficult relationship you should spend more time with.

Temptation bundling uses the instant gratification one receives with the fun activity to help either start or engage in the second, less fun activity.

It works so well that she decided to test the theory out and published the findings in a paper titled "holding the hunger games hostage at the gym," which was published in management science.

She split her subjects into three groups. The first group was given an iPod loaded with books that were known to be exciting reads. They kept the iPod at the gym and were not allowed to take it home. They could listen to the novels only during their 30 minute workout. If it ended on a cliffhanger, they needed to wait until the next scheduled workout.

The second group situation was slightly different. These iPods were also loaded with the same novels, but they could take them home and if they wanted. They would need to exercise willpower if they were to only listen while working out.

The last group was the control. They were given a gift certificate to Barnes & Noble and told to exercise for 30 minutes at the beginning of the study. They could listen to anything they wanted to do at the gym and were told to simply exercise more.

The researchers followed the three groups for nine weeks. The first group exercised 51% more frequently than the control group, while the second group exercised 29% more frequently.

This is profound and shows that this technique really works.

How do you do it for yourself?

Start with two lists. One is the stuff you like doing your guilty pleasures if you will. Watching a favorite TV show, surfing the Internet, playing a videogame, browsing social media, etc. The choices here are going to be plentiful.

The second list is the stuff you tend to

procrastinate on: cleaning the house, washing the dishes, exercising, eating healthy, getting organized, etc.

Look for ways to combine those two lists. For example, you will only listen to your favorite music when you were washing the dishes or you can watch TV shows that you love when you're exercising. Something that ties the two together.

If you do that you will see huge gains. The possibilities are endless. However, the principal remains the same, use the first activity to encourage the second one.

It leads to consistency which is one of the most important aspect of self-discipline. Like they say, showing up is half the battle.

These small, regular victories give you confidence because you're hitting her goals in a regular basis.

It leads to mastery in your chosen area. James Clear also states that something worth mentioning in his article and temptation bundling and that is this, the most important tasks are never urgent.

In other words, if you miss a workout it is not the

end world, however, if you begin to consistently miss workouts then your health begins to decline over time.

Cleaning or decluttering your office may not seem like a big deal but it leads to a clear mind and better organization.

Utilizing temptation bundling well to become the person you want to become.

There are many ways to go about this. I just listed a few. If you take the time and really look at what is important to you and what you're not getting done and combine it with an enjoyable task, you will find your life improving in ways you never could have imagined,

only because you are now being consistent with your time.

Chapter 7. The One Thing

When we begin to think about time management, self-discipline, success, oftentimes, when we are asked to define them. It becomes very difficult. I'm talking about the more subjective areas such as what is success to you?

Basically what we want is to figure out from the top down. What is important? Gary Keller and Jay Papasan in 'The One Thing the surprisingly simple truth behind extraordinary results' lays out the case that long to do lists and multitasking are huge obstacles in our quest to accomplish our goals.

The authors state that you will achieve extraordinary success from focusing on "One Thing" by developing superior focus. By aligning your purpose with that focus you will become unstoppable by only having one priority.

Make a success list and use that to chart your course.

Block out time to accomplish those items that

contribute to the bottom line of the one thing you want to accomplish.

Do not agree to take on other projects or say yes to items and things that will take your time away and your focus away from becoming the best you can be in that one thing that you have defined as important to you.

I call this working from the top down. By taking a 10,000 foot view of your life and determining at that view what is truly important, you can zero in on the priorities to make your life better.

When you do this you will not be pulled in many different directions, trying to figure out what is a priority and what isn't.

This new world of social media and 24 hour Internet access has turned off the filter of what is important and what is not important. Everything seems important nowadays. And it can be difficult to separate and categorize the most important to least important because it seems as if everyone is shouting from the rooftops the importance of their product for your specific situation and how it and only it can save you from whatever disaster lurks around the corner.

Does it sound familiar? If you look online for a solution to a particular problem you will find workshops, video courses, e-classrooms and everything else there is devoted to solving that specific problem. Can you see why you're overwhelmed with everything? Everyone has a something to sell you that will make all of your problems go away. Heck, before you read it you probably didn't know you even had the problem, right?

By focusing on your goal, focusing on your mission in this life you will begin to automatically cut away the unimportant, the clutter and will be able to get down to the bare essence of what is important.

If we start here, this is the reason I put this at the beginning of the book, we will see massive improvements in our self-discipline, our goal attainment, and our quality of life.

Forget the lies you've been told that everything matters equally.

It doesn't.

We make our decisions quickly and without thinking them through properly because we have too much to do and too many things to focus on.

When you narrow it down to just a few things you will make better decisions and you will have better peace of mind. It will make self-discipline effortless too because you will cut down on decision fatigue which is another drain on your already finite willpower.

You also need to get rid of multitasking.

Multitasking does not work. Study after study has shown that when your attention is divided, the quality of your work goes down exponentially as Steve Guzzo is quoted in the One Thing says "It gives you the ability to quote screw up more than one thing at a time."

The other thing it does slows down your work switching from task to task takes away your energy and eats up your workday.

Concentrate on one thing at a time.

I know this may sound counterintuitive to this book, but you will see later on what I am talking about, but self-discipline is overrated.

Does that strike a chord with you? Good, that means I have your attention.

Here is why self-discipline is overrated. You trying to achieve your goals through sheer force of will.

By putting all of your effort and willpower into certain activities or goals that you feel will get you ahead and constantly striving and working towards something that you want to accomplish, you are concentrating all of your willpower into that goal to get you there. This is not optimal or sustainable.

What willpower is great for, is for establishing habits that will get you there. Later on in this book we will discuss how to establish these habits and how to go about creating the ones you need in order to accomplish the goal at hand.

But for now just keep in mind what I said about willpower and self-discipline.

Willpower, as I just mentioned, is a finite resource that we only have so much of if you rely on it to get you through you are going to be extremely disappointed and always wonder why things are not working out and why you don't have the discipline to accomplish what you want to accomplish.

Rest assured, if this has been your problem you are in for a paradigm shift in your thinking.

Chapter 8. Marshmallow Test

Willpower gets a bad rap.

People blame lack of willpower on everything from obesity to poor career choices to not making enough money. Carl Eric Fisher warns us against this. Don't oversimplify the message. There are many factors that contribute to self-control and he urges people to stop over emphasizing the importance of willpower in his excellent book Against Willpower.

Eric explains why the concept willpower is simplistic and inaccurate and why our obsession with it can be toxic when someone over rates its importance.

They ignore other things such as emotional regulation and intrapersonal bargaining.

By reevaluating the importance of willpower in our lives, it can help us shine a different light on some of society's problems.

Fisher readily admits that the idea of ignoring willpower will sound crazy to most people. However, as an addiction psychiatrist and a clinical professor of psychiatry, he became very suspect and skeptical about the importance of willpower even when it is and he focused in on the self-help industries fascination with it.

Willpower finds its roots in early Christianity where it is celebrated as a virtue. However, researchers and scientists such as BF Skinner suggested that we as human beings have little control over our impulses instead focused on behaviorism. In other words, people learn their behaviors and how to act putting willpower on the back burner. An excellent study in the 1960s was called the marshmallow test.

If you haven't heard about it here's what happened.

Walter Mischel conducted an experiment with children to measure delayed gratification. He placed a child in a room by themselves with a plate of marshmallows in front of them.

Hence the name of the test, The Marshmallow Experiment.

___

This test was conducted at Stanford University in 1960 by Walter Mischel. The purpose of the study was to gain a better understanding of delayed gratification.

In other words, the ability to wait for something better than the alternative placed in front of them.

At the being nursery school located at Stanford University children aged 4 to 6 years age years of age were led into a room that contained no distractions. On a plate, were treats such as a marshmallow or a cookie, etc. The children were told that they could eat that marshmallow right then, but if they waited 15 minutes and they didn't eat it. They would get a second treat.

The results were fascinating of the children 600 in total, only a few of them ate the marshmallow immediately.

Of the ones that wanted to wait, only 1/3 were able to defer gratification long enough to get that second treat.

There were 16 boys and 16 girls and in follow-up studies, the preschool children who delayed gratification the longest were found to be, by their parent's observations, more competent or able to accomplish goals better and led to higher SAT scores and even in further studies showed that they were able to attain higher education and better jobs.

Here's something that's interesting about that, if a child had been shown before that by their parents that if in some way that if they were to wait, they would end up with a treat. They were more likely to follow through and be able to wait. However, if they had been shown in the past, to not have a prize waiting for them at the end of the 15 minute period, then they would not wait. They would have a very difficult time waiting for their treat. This makes sense because if you if the child has not been shown that waiting 15 minutes for an additional treat would have a benefit, or if they were put into circumstances where the benefit would manifest itself randomly, then they will have learned that behavior.

I believe there are certain misconceptions drawn from the study. If it is only taken at first blush, and not looked at in its entirety. The fact of the matter is this type of control or this type of behavior can be learned. This leads into other areas, such as back in the chapter were we spoke about just do something by accomplishing small goals. You are conditioning yourself to success, no matter how small it may seem at the time the fact the matter is, your brain is getting a little push of dopamine each time it accomplishes a small goal. This will in turn lead to bigger and bigger goals, allowing you to accomplish two things at one time: not grow too quick, and to expect progress giving you confidence.

This is what is important about that - by allowing yourself to obtain small victories on a regular basis, you will transform how you approach problems. You will not be overwhelmed and you will see progress. This is what you need in order to see progress and in order to grow into your dream job dream career or whatever it is. It could be anything sport, it could be a lot of different things, but by giving yourself this training your mind conditioned to victory and it will give you that edge you need in life.

Chapter 9. Your Purpose

In order to develop self-discipline, you need to define what is important to you, what are you looking for? Is it a new career, a new skill? Maybe you want to develop aspects of your personality that you want to change?

Ben Settle in his book, Persuasion Secrets of the World's Most Charismatic and Influential villains, takes a tongue-in-cheek approach to explaining this. He uses the villain as the most influential and charismatic individual in the story and makes a compelling case for it.

Why am I talking about this?

The reason I bring it up is to illustrate the point of how important it is to be able to have a mission in your life. Something greater then yourself that allows you to dream about and to shoot for.

While his book is highly entertaining and informative, the reality is it's also very true.

This falls under finding your mission.

When you find your mission. Self-discipline becomes automatic.

The reason why is because it is necessary to accomplish the mission in front of you.

Only you know what your mission is it is very personal.

It is the overriding passion you have for something that makes you go into a zone when you're working at it.

It could be a sport or a creative pursuit such as music. Whatever it is, you go after it with everything you have.

You would do it for free. That's how much you are into it.

So in order to become the best in your chosen field and the best is relative to what you want to accomplish. I maybe should phrase it as the best to your ability, then you are going to need a certain skill set to apply to your mission.

Now you will not look at this is an isolated pursuit.

It is part of the system that you are putting in place to accomplish the goal you set out for yourself in order for you to grow and accomplish your mission in life.

Let's put some things in perspective; there is no one looking out for you. You are reading this book because you want to develop self-discipline. But why? It's because you know deep down inside that in order for you to accomplish what you were put here on this earth for you need to first control yourself.

If you don't, someone will gladly step in and take over that role. It could be a boss, it could be a needy girlfriend or boyfriend, overbearing friends, the list goes on and on. If you do not control what your mission is in life, someone else will dictate it for you so that they can accomplish their goals.

That's not what you want.

That is not why you are on this earth and it is up to you to determine how your life goes.

You understand this at a cellular level. It may not

be conscious but it's there. Something is telling you from the recesses of your subconscious that you need to be in control of your own life.

Do your future self a favor and adopt this attitude going forward.

We live for our future selves to accomplish what we should be trying to accomplish today. Don't let that happen anymore. It is a habit that is very difficult to break, and you need to break it in order to get things done. That is why I keep advocating that you start small so that you can accomplish small goals which lead to bigger and bigger ones.

Another word you can substitute mission for is your purpose.

Studies have shown that individuals with a high sense of purpose, along with feeling like they are in control lived longer, have less disease and have make more money and have better relationships than those that don't.

This was conducted over 8 1/2 years in follow-up.

If that isn't a strong enough message for you to develop purpose in your life. I don't know what to tell you.

At Very Well Mind, blog, Amy Moran lays out seven things to develop in your life that will lead to finding your purpose in helping you develop self-discipline you want in order to accomplish your mission or purpose in life.

1.   Donating time, money, or talent. All of these are good. I would recommend that if you have the opportunity to devote time to a project. Please try to do that. The feeling you will get from being present in the situation and helping people out is second to none. Giving money is great, but time is one of things you will look back on and you will remember it and have a very good feeling from it. Money comes and goes.

2.   Listen to feedback. Sometimes you do not know what is important to you. Ask friends or loved ones for insight. You are more than likely displaying a passion for something that is been so ingrained in you that you don't even realize you are doing it. Take note when someone mentions something you do that they like or appreciate. Do not underestimate what they say underestimate what they say.

3.   Surround yourself with uplifting people. You are a composite of the top five people you spend the most time with an Amy Moran explains

that you need to be careful who you surround yourself with because you will become like the people you are around the most. If you aspire to be successful. Place yourself around people that have already attained the success that you are looking for. Negativity will drag you down.

4.   Start conversations with new people. Be open to new opportunities as they present themselves to you. Everyone has a story. Find out about them and what their interests are. It will help you develop patience and active listening. It will open your eyes to new experiences and you never know, you may end up in the career of your dreams are with the partner of your dreams. It can help you discover and newfound sense of purpose for something you may have dismissed before. You never know.

5.   Explore your interests. What you spend the most time thinking about? What do you spend the most time talking about with good friends, when you discover this you can find out what truly inspires you and help you better understand your true purpose.

6.   Injustices that make you mad. Do you hate animal abuse, are you an advocate for MADD - Mothers Against Drunk Driving? Has a loved one suffered a horrific crime and you felt powerless to

help. Maybe it is too big to tackle all by yourself. It you know of an organization devoted to fighting that particular injustice and you devote your time and resources to helping our organization. It doesn't matter just find something you care about and do something to help, you will feel better.

7.   What do you love? Consider your skills and passions and find out where they intersect. Maybe you're a bookkeeper or accountant who was a whiz with numbers and maybe you are passionate about helping an animal shelter, so volunteer your time and talents to balance their books, anything. Use your imagination and creativity to think of fun ways to help others. You are the one that benefits from this more than they ever will. It sounds selfish but it isn't. By giving of yourself and giving of your time and your talents you are helping others, which feels so good and it's so good for you.

It will take some time to find your purpose and don't worry if you don't have it all figured out at once. By simply taking action on the steps listed above you will be well on your way to finding it and changing your life.

Chapter 10. Win the Morning!

Do you want to become more disciplined? Of course you do, you are reading this book after all, and you've gotten this far.

But what we've learned up to this point is all well and good. You say. But how do we apply these concepts you've talked about into our lives so that we can make better decisions and develop better self-discipline?

Yes, you can see the potential for breakthroughs but now how do you put it all together?

Is this you? You wake up and immediately check your phone?

You scroll your social media site of choice, get caught up on what happened overnight since you last checked it and then do a quick check of your email only to become stressed out because an emergency or something bad is waiting for you at work and now you have to think about it before you get there.

Worse yet, you begin responding to the emails believing there needs to be an immediate response.

Perhaps you hit the snooze button a few times and finally dragged yourself out of bed already running late and behind schedule.

Now you have this vision of your day ahead of you with you behind and chronically late and anxious.

How long did all of that take? 15 minutes 10? Not too long, really. In that time however, you have set yourself up for failure.

What if there was a different way?

The trick is to start the habit of a morning routine. So much has been written about the morning routine from Richard Branson, CEO of Virgin Atlantic, Steve Jobs, to Benjamin Franklin. All of these people have espoused the importance of starting their day on the right foot.

It has also been championed by Hal Elrod, the creator of the Miracle Morning where he lays out

—

some simple steps to increase personal development but he isn't the only one that is using this to accomplish it. He just happened to come up with a very, very effective way of explaining it that has hit at the heart of the matter with many people

.

Why start a morning routine? Studies show an increase in motivation, decreased anxiety and depression and stress with people who were considered early risers or morning people. The affect was the same with both younger and older demographics.

Studies have also shown that are most productive time is two hours after we wake up. Having a structure in place you will set yourself up for success by hitting your stride at the right time.

You will also make better decisions.

By giving yourself small victories in the morning because you followed your morning routine, you will now have a better mindset to tackle the difficult task that will come up later in your workday if you want this for yourself.

You do not necessarily need to get up at 5 AM every day to enjoy the benefits.

By putting together a morning routine that includes some key ingredients we will go over in a while you can gain a crucial advantage over your old self.

Here are some of the benefits you can expect from a solid morning routine:

Physical: by starting your day with some form of physical exercise, and it does not have to be much, you give your body a rush of endorphins right off the bat, making you feel great. At the same time it's improving your health in the crucial incremental 1% improvement that we've talked about already. It can be as simple as doing yoga stretches all the way to going to the gym. It's up to you.

Mental: a more centered self. Sitting down to meditate or journaling can have profound impacts on your ability to keep a clear mind. The simple process of writing has been shown to decrease anxiety and depression because the brain can actually work out or at least have the sensation of working out the problem just by putting it into words on paper or typing it onto a screen. It gives you an outlet. Meditation does the same thing because now you are aware of your thoughts and you are not judging your situation the way you would normally do it when you are in the middle of the situation. By being silent and allowing your thoughts to come and go, and to quiet your mind you center yourself. Do both of these things, meditation and journaling and you can become unstoppable.

It also gives you a few minutes of time to yourself on a regular basis. By giving yourself a structured time every day to focus on yourself and do something in the morning when you're most productive. You get 10 times more stuff done on a regular basis and this can have a compound effect on your life. Hal Elrod talks about going from nearly bankrupt and nearly homeless to making an over six-figure per year job in under two months.

Also by doing so you will see that your you have decrease stress and anxiety because you got the important items done in the morning before everyone else got up. It gives you the structure to begin your day as well as the rest of the day as well.

I know what you're going to ask next, what if I am not a morning person?

Many people claim they are not. This is where mindset comes in. You were not going to become a morning person overnight. You will need to employ some tactics to work up to this.

Here are a few.

1.   Go to bed 15 minutes earlier. Psychologically, it will be easier to then get up 15 minutes earlier. That's really all you need to begin an effective morning routine.

2.   Use the five second rule. Mel Robbin's book the five second rule shows a very simple way to get out of bed easier by simply counting backwards from five down to zero. Much like a rocket launch. It may sound silly but it works and is backed by science. What you are doing is activating the prefrontal cortex to overwrite the indecision or lack of willpower to get out of bed.Try it, you will be surprised how well it worked. By just taking action. It puts your plan into motion. And having an established morning routine to look forward to. After getting up will set you up for success.

Okay, so we've established the fact that we need a morning routine.

But what should go into this morning routine?

We've already touched on a few things previously...

Going to each one a bit further –

Meditation. The benefits of been covered in the foundational chapter. Start small. Work your way up to 10 minutes a day but start with a minute. Journaling morning pages by Julia Cameron is a journaling style or one writes three pages per day. It is very effective at working out the problems you are facing or believe you are facing and is extremely therapeutic. The act of journaling has been proven in research to eliminate depression and anxiety.

Gratitude write down three things you are grateful for every day. Again covered elsewhere in this book, but when you start out thankful for loved ones and situations in your life, you can become successful. It does not work the other way around, though. You cannot become successful then become thankful.

Light exercise – yoga, stretching a walk. All of these things work together to get your heart rate up, thus improving your health and giving you clarity for other tasks as they come up.

You can add whatever else you want and personalize it to your tastes and needs. I know people who study martial arts who want to learn certain moves and will study that particular sequence and review it so they can apply it to the next time they train.

The possibilities are endless, but try to have the core elements outlined above. Other than that your needs and wants, etc. will vary. Start small and workup to both the routine and getting up early if you are not an early riser.

What if the morning routine is not working?

Look at your bedtime routine.

We all have one and it usually involves doing something on your phone or watching TV.

This is something you want to avoid, especially computer screens of all type a couple hours before bed because they emit blue light, which can disrupt your melatonin production, leading to decreased and non-restful sleep.

Try to read a physical book with light instead of looking at your screen or if you have to wear a pair blue light filtering computer glasses. Research has shown the glasses to filter out the harmful effects of the blue light. Better to stay away from them. The screens that is, but the glasses are worth a shot and see if that helps.

Track your time. Find out what is empty time and eliminated. Like junk food, empty time can lead to bloat, which does not lead to productivity. You will find that it will be easier to get to bed earlier because you've cut out nonessential activities.

Knowing your why. As we discussed in a previous chapter. This is key and we all know this because if you know why you're getting up in the morning. It makes everything else easier everything stems from your why.

What are you trying to accomplish? What is the overriding goal here? When you know the answer to that question. Everything else will begin to fall into place.

Chapter 11. Self-Compassion and Self-Discipline

Which is better, high self-esteem or humility?

Something that gets lost in our quest to develop greater self-discipline in our lives is the notion of being kind to ourselves.

The fact of the matter is this, you are going to slip up and you are going to procrastinate even though you have made the commitment to becoming a better time manager. It happens and it is OK.

What may in fact be holding you back is the way you talk to yourself when you slip up.

Why go for big goals if you are just going to be scolded and given a lecture about how you always do this and will never amount to anything?

Who is giving this talk? Yourself.

It is coming from inside of you because you do not understand any other way to approach dealing with setbacks.

Let me ask you, would you tell a good friend or family member the same thing if you were to see them cheat on their diet? Or saw a them scrolling through their social media feed when they said they were going to be studying?

If you are a good friend you would gently remind them but only if they asked you to beforehand. No, you would be kind to them.

So why can't we be the same way to ourselves?

Kristen Neff lays out some of the myths surrounding self-compassion.

1. Self-Compassion is a form of self-pity. In other words, feeling sorry for yourself. In actuality, it is the antidote to self-pity. You are not tuning out bad stuff or glossing it over, what it does is makes you accept, experience, and acknowledge hard feelings with grace and tolerance. People with high levels of self-compassion are not as likely to fall into self-pity as others who are harder on themselves. They are also less likely to experience anxiety or depression.

2. Self-Compassion means weakness. Often when are faced with something as devastating as infidelity being betrayed by someone we trusted the guard come up and will not come down. No way you are going to let someone in and see you vulnerable under any circumstances. However, research has shown that self-compassion is one of the most powerful ways of dealing with a major crisis in our lives. Research has been conducted looking at recently divorced people who were graded on the type self talk they conducted during a stream of consciousness recording. Later on during follow up the found that the people who displayed the most self compassion towards the divorce and towards their partner had a better psychological rebound and was still there nine months later. The point of this was to show that what truly matters is how you face the obstacles put in your life and how you treat yourself when the chips are down.

3. Self-compassion will make me complacent. Like a sadistic coach screaming at you to 'Just gut it out' and 'C'mon soldier, you better not let me down!' One of the biggest obstacles to self compassion is that it will undercut our ability to persevere or push ourselves to be better. The thought is if we do not criticize ourselves to press on then we will just give up and not go after the goal or do it half heartedly. However, like I wrote earlier in this chapter, would you do the same thing to your child if they came home after failing a test? Of course you wouldn't. Not to say that you wouldn't

recognize the fact that the grade needs to come up but you would be more likely to frame it in such a way so that your child learns to adopt better study habits and to ask for help beforehand. So why don't we do that with ourselves? Why is it that when we fail we succumb to negative self-talk? Take the same approach you would take with a loved one and acknowledge that things need to change but that there is always an opportunity to change it. Research is showing more and more that self-compassion will actually strengthen personal accountability. What it gives you is much needed objectiveness. When you are in the middle of something you are experiencing you lose that. Self-compassion gives you the objectiveness you need and to put things in perspective so that you can get up, dust yourself off, and try again.

4. Self-compassion is narcissistic. In fact, self compassion is nothing like overly high self esteem. Self-esteem is something that can be fleeting and goes up and down based on the situation in front of you. If you are good at something and surrounded by others who are just learning that particular skill, you can feel very high levels of self esteem, however change the situation and take your same skill level in a room full of experts in that particular skill and you may not feel the same shine you did previously. Self compassion on the other hand is not based on how you feel at that particular moment. It is how you relate to how things are around you and things could be changing by the second. For example if you mess

something up for someone else you can apologize to them, do your best to fix it, then tell yourself that these things happen and you will do better next time. That's it. No beating yourself up. High self-compassion leads to greater emotional stability regardless of the circumstances or how much or how little praise they receive for something.

5. Self-compassion is selfish. It can be interpreted as taking resources away from helping others and using it on yourself. Neff asks if compassion is a zero-sum game? She makes the argument that when you are absorbed in self-pity you actually have less to give others. She calls it a paradoxical form of self-centeredness. By meeting our own emotional needs first we are in a better position to help others. She states that women fall into this trap a lot by trying so hard to be everything to everyone else they end. This leads to them trying to balance everything and be everything to everyone especially if they have a demanding career. However it is not limited to women. Men can fall into this as well especially if there is a change in their ability to provide, i.e. they lose a job or get demoted etc. By having a high level of self-compassion we are in a better position to be loving spouses, parents, and friends.

So what does all of this have to do with self-discipline?

The answer is simple. As you adopt new habits to

increase your self-discipline you are going to run into obstacles and setbacks. By forgiving yourself and showing that you are your own biggest cheerleader you will be more likely to stick with your new found habits and your goals will be that much closer.

Chapter 12. 80/20 Guide. Pareto Principle

Do you want to know the secret to accomplishing great goals?

The answer may surprise you. In fact what I'm about to suggest will maybe strike a chord with you and make you think I am crazy.

I assure you I am not.

What I'm going to recommend, is for you to do less.

That's correct less.

In order to maximize your best efforts, you need to concentrate them and by concentrating them on better outcomes you accomplish what you set out to accomplish.

You will find that it is better for your health, for

your stress levels, for your relationships with loved ones, and for everything else that matters to you.

What I am talking about was identified by Vifredo Pareto, who made the distinction that 80% of Italy's land was owned by 20% of the population.

He began looking at other countries and found this to be true in every instance that he looked. It was the same distribution pattern in effect.

The Pareto principle looked at processes in just about every field from engineering to sociology, economy, politics, anything you could basically think of the vast majority of time, the competition for resources was dominated by 20% in some cases it may even more pronounced.

So what does this mean to you? How can you apply this to your life to make things better to move ahead at an accelerated pace and identify the tasks and functions you do that are the most important to your job. For example, if your job is that of an accountant, you will be better served working on client work that gives you income other tasks such as answering the phone, responding to emails, and all of the other functions that happen in an office which would probably be better utilized by hiring someone to come in and perform those duties for you so you can spend your attention and resources on the things that matter to your bottom line.

This also works in sports. In the sport of Brazilian jujitsu there are literally thousands of moves that can be performed to subdue an opponent. However, there is an almost disparaging number of times in high level tournaments that one very basic move that a new practitioner will learn within several months of beginning training can use at even the highest levels. For example, if in a match, the opponent winds up on the back of the other opponent and chokes the person or submits him or her. They have found that particular move is utilized and successful in more than 60 to 70% of matches at the highest level. In other words, the 80/20 rule works here as well. It shows that just a handful of moves in each position will yield nearly all of the results versus the other moves combined.

Somewhere else this can be looked at is in the field of politics. Politics such as in the American system, the party of the Republicans and the Democrats dominates the political scene.

There are hundreds of other private parties such as Libertarians, the Green party, the Communist Party, the socialist party, and on and on and on but we never hear anything about them. They never make a strong run for party dominance, except maybe at the local level. At the national level, it will always be between the two major parties and everyone else is a very distant second. By taking this principle and applying it to your work. I believe it is easy to see just how important this principle is going forward. Do not focus on the busywork in front of you and on the long to do list you have written in your daytime or on your calendar program on your phone. Instead, focus only on the tasks they give you the most bang for your buck. You will know what they are and they are specific to you but if you follow this as I've laid out.

I believe you will make significant progress and it makes self-discipline that much easier because now you are only focusing in on a few different habits to give yourself. You are not focusing on the entire picture of productivity and self-discipline, instead what you are focusing on are just a couple of different things that will get you ahead in the fastest amount of time possible.

You can apply to developing self-discipline as well. Instead of making a huge list of foods you can't eat, instead focus on just a few foods that you know are healthful and tasty. You do not have to think about the myriad choices that abound and simply focus on the few that give you the most benefit. Or, you can use a simple rule that says you will always have a protein source in each meal. This simplifies things.

How about batching your email and only checking it once or twice a day? You will save time and energy as well as be more productive by cutting your email response time down to 20% of your time instead of the 80% you may be spending now.

Try making goals that cut across different disciplines of your life. Becoming a better listener can help you become a better spouse, parent, manager, business owner. Getting to be a better budgeter can help you at home and at your job.

So by adopting a few key habits you can have profound impact in many different areas of your life instead of adopting a bunch of new habits.

Chapter 13. Look for Micro Improvements

1% Improvement. It may not seem like much, but the fact of the matter is we are either improving or declining a little each and every day.

If you look at as an X and Y axis aligned going straight up and going straight across. If you put your life right in the middle going parallel to the X axis. You can see that there will be either gradual trend upwards or gradual trends downwards.

This can be discouraging, if you look at it wrong.

You may think 'I don't have control over that, that is just the way my life is going.'

Or it can be sobering if you truly see how the little things you do each day will add up no matter what. They can be good or bad, they do not judge.

The process is called aggregate gains. It is the

compound effect of either a good or a bad habit.

Let's look at several examples. If you never miss a workout then over time, the aggregate gain will be solid fitness.

Let's say your nutrition is something you struggle with and continue to make poor food choices day in and day out, you will find yourself overweight and with preventable diseases such as heart disease and diabetes.

Small wins and slow gains, according to James Clear are the goal. The system is where it is at and you need to master your habits. Do not aim for huge changes all at once.

Having huge goals is wonderful but it is also intimidating and can actually bring down your enthusiasm. Eventually it will lead to inaction and over analysis and you will develop difficulty making progress. The little things will stress you and make you uncomfortable and zap your energy.

Set small goals, create a system for accomplishing that small goal and experience the win.

Make the process the goal.

What you do not want to do is this. Don't think about the big picture all the time, simply use that as a rudder towards where you were going.

Pretend you are swimming in a lake and headed toward an island in the middle of a lake. Will you get impatient if you are not at the lake within a certain amount of time? Will you tell yourself that you should have been there already? Of course not, you will get there when you get there. However, if you look up occasionally to see if you're on track and not headed in the wrong direction that is okay. The goal is simply something you are aiming for, the swimming is the key. Concentrating on smooth strokes, conserving your energy etc are the immediate goals that will get you to the island. Concentrating on anything else and you can drown.

You just do not want to become consumed with the idea of not accomplishing your goal. You are moving toward your goal and are making progress, even if it does not feel like it because the water is deep and cold.

James Clear also says to focus on the daily process and enjoy the present moment and succeed.

It is called the kaizen approach, which is Japanese for continuous improvement.

It emphasizes making small improvements each

day. Think of the smallest step you can take every day to achieve that goal. It can be as simple as sending an email to a potential client, even if it is not hundred percent perfect. Or making a phone call to someone that you haven't spoken to in a long time and you need to mend that fence.

Big business is doing this. General Electric collects and analyzes data from its vast areas of operation and uses it to make micro improvements in efficiency. This is, according to Greg Wells at entrepreneur magazine, been documented as a huge success. They have made these improvements over time and the results speak for themselves.

Like we discussed in the foundational habits chapter, if you are not getting enough sleep. Try to improve going to bed 15 minutes earlier than usual for a week then increase it until you are getting the optimal amount you need.

Poor nutrition? Try adding a protein source to each meal to counteract the other less desirable carbohydrates present.

So even if you aren't ready to completely alter your diet at least you're getting something a little more nutritionally sound to begin with. While you're at it, try to cut down on the empty calories. It leaves room for more healthy options.

Take the stairs for one flight of your journey to the office and then take the elevator for the rest, if your condition doesn't allow you to take the entire stairs to your office.

Meditate for one minute a day to start. You're more than likely to stay with that if you do this, increase it as needed.

Let's put some things in perspective. If you were to improve one thing 1% each day. Where would you end up? Laura Stack lays it out nicely. She says if you can improve 1% each day you would roughly double your ability every 70 days.

Think about the possibilities here. It is mind boggling. Just doing something 1% better each day. You will be a new person in a little over two months in that particular area.

For instance, let's say you want to listen to your spouse better just 1%. Imagine that if you did this your relationship with him or her would get better and better instead of possibly drifting apart with nothing to talk about.

Too often we try to do things when it's too late. We are already in over our head and we get overwhelmed.

With this 1% improvement mantra. We can take on huge projects and not be overwhelmed by them.

Just sit back right now and think about one thing you want to get better at.

Got it?

Now think about the smallest incremental step you can take to accomplish. It falls in line with the first principles thinking we already spoke about in that chapter.

It gives you the best chance of becoming the disciplined person you want to be. The person who does what they say they are going to do, no matter what.

Say for instance you want to become more punctual begin getting ready five minutes earlier than you would normally begin getting ready.

Will you still be late? Maybe, but maybe not as late

and as time goes on, you'll begin to see that you are becoming more and more punctual. This is the goal, it's not all at once.

The change doesn't happen instantaneously. It happens gradually and in time. All of a sudden, you begin seeing yourself as a punctual person if not early to appointments.

Devin from Project No Limits on YouTube wrote or says success is not overnight. It is a daily commitment. Think about old apprenticeships. They would work daily until they became proficient and eventually would become the master of their trade. For example, blacksmiths.

Improving your life is as easy as 1%. The first step is to look for at every opportunity is a way to improve. Perhaps you get mad when someone says something to you that triggers you, maybe now you decide I'm going to count to 10 before I respond.

What will this do? It gives you a second to think now to not react like you had and all of a sudden you're reacting to things 1% better than you did.

Or let's say you can take a little things such as eye contact. Say you want to hold eye contact better with people and noticed a change in the conversations that you have with those people. Are they improving? I'm sure they are and it may not even be noticeable, but they are.

Maybe improve your posture. Stand up a little straighter and it will seem like you are better overnight from doing that?

Of course not, but what it does is gives you the ability to stand up straighter and with that posture improvement you feel better.

Another thing you can do read five pages a day, you'll learn something new each and every day and you will become more interesting to other people around you. You will also become smarter and learn more things and be more disciplined and you'll finish more books.

Do this for a year when you think happens?

Do you get 365% better if you did 1% improvement each day for a year? The answer will surprise you, and that is no, you will not get 365% better.

What you will get is a thousand to 2000% better

because the effects compound each other.

They build upon each other. It's like compound interest in your finances.

How do you get started? Look at small areas. Organize something in your life that is bugging you. Maybe there's a bookshelf or your desk that is messy.

Clean it and all of a sudden you are feeling more like the person that cleans their workspace and works in a clean, organized environment. Perhaps now you are known as the person who is organized and maybe you weren't before.

Do it day in and day out.

Write down the one thing you want to start with 1% improvement on a Post-it note commit to doing it for three days.

Do this and see where you're at in a year's time. If you stick with it. I can almost guarantee you your life will change for the better and dramatically.

Chapter 14. Why Constraints are Necessary

Constraints and self-discipline. It is easy to tell ourselves that we don't have the time for the energy or the skills or the connections to accomplish the goals we set for ourselves.

These self-imposed constraints, real or otherwise, can keep you in an endless loop of wanting something, feeling that the universe is conspiring against you, and preventing you from obtaining what you want.

However, there is a better way to look at this.

View the constraint as something good. How can not having something help us become better at a skill? Here is why, it forces you to develop the skill that would otherwise go undeveloped, because you did not have that constraint in place in the first place.

What this means is simple.

If, for example, you do not like getting up early but you want to develop the habit of getting up early. You have now forced yourself into a time constraint giving you the option of waking up and starting your day earlier than before.

I recommend trying things in very small chunks and I also recommend making whatever goal you want to accomplish very specific.

Let's stay with our example. You want to establish the habit of getting up earlier, say 6 AM every day so that you are not rushing out the door to get to work and you can have time to either read, meditate, write, whatever it is you are missing out on because you are starting your day behind the eight ball and late.

By giving yourself just one week, you are giving yourself the best chance of obtaining the goal of getting up earlier with less chance of failure.

Also by committing to one week, if that particular goal is not right for you, you can stick it out for seven days and then decide that you may want to try something else.

Perhaps it is a specific skill you want to develop and not a behavior.

I know I wanted to develop the skill of writing daily. What does it take to become a better writer? Very simple but not easy. One needs to write consistently. If I get up first thing in the morning and write down whatever it is I decide to write that morning, generally it is just a brain dump, I find that writing other things is much easier.

By writing daily, the ability becomes much more effortless and second nature, which makes me extend my goal. So now instead of seven days. I will commit to two weeks and then three and then four until it is a daily habit and something as natural to me as brushing my teeth.

James Clear says focus on something you want to develop. Make it very specific. For example, you cannot tell yourself you want to be good at business or communication.

Both of these skills are broad topics they are not skills per se. They are areas to master and very broad and general.

Instead, do this, tell yourself, 'I want to make 25 phone calls every morning before 8 AM to potential clients.'

It does not matter if every call hangs up on you.

You are developing the necessary skill to become better at that facet of business.

You can then carry that over into other areas of your business, such as becoming better at business accounting or bookkeeping so that you know where your money is going. It can go on and on like this. As you develop each skill you get stronger in your field.

Another example would be to say I want to be good at communication. What does that mean exactly? Communication can range from delivered speeches to a crowd of people all the way down to a text message from a friend saying they are running late.

What you do instead is say I want to sit down with my spouse every Wednesday at 8 o'clock after the kids have gone to bed and discuss items we don't normally get to discuss because we are so busy.

This will improve the relationship as well as improve your communication skills. You can even take it one step further and say during that time, I am going to be a better listener and truly empathize with my partner so that he or she can see that I truly understand where he or she is coming from.

You can then extend this open communication skill into other areas as well such as work, where you may want to say, I want to discuss this project with my boss in a positive and constructive manner. Perhaps this is a touchy area and you and your boss have clashed over it in the past.

Make it a game. Look at the constraints you have as obstacles in a videogame that you need to get past. Mario, of the popular Nintendo games does not complain as he makes his way through the various constraints placed in front of him as he tries to rescue the princess. No, he takes each one and overcomes them as they pop up. You can do the same. You won't see it as something holding you back and it will make it much funner for you to attempt. You are simply playing within the rules of the game now. By reframing the problem into this light. You have shown yourself that you can accomplish goals in the process of developing self-discipline becomes much more fun.

There are only three things that can be manipulated to develop the specific skill you want to develop time, resources, and your environment.

Let's take a look at each constraint and see how we

can make them work for us.

Time, this resource is usually everyone's biggest obstacle. Let's say your boss gives you a project that is due in one month. The old way of doing it, as Albert Einstein says, would be to allow the time given and use up every second of it until it is due within 30 days.

How about giving yourself a self-imposed deadline of seven days? See what happens, I think you will be surprised.

Resources, if you travel pack light, put everything you will take on that trip into one carry-on bag or a backpack. This forces you to break it down into the bare essentials. It also frees you up considerably to be able to move in a much more relaxed way because you are not worried about your luggage being lost or having to carry heavy suitcases everywhere you go.

Your environment. Let's say you work with access to the Internet. It can be a giant time suck and is limitless in its ability to induce dopamine rushes of intense euphoria as you search and forage for newer and better information.

How about turning it off and not checking it at all

while you are engaged in whatever project you happen to be doing, whether it be at work or at home? Make your office a no go zone for technology other than say your word processing or spreadsheet document.

What do you want to become good at? What is important to you and to your career to turn it into the life that you want developed?

Sit down and really think about these things. Give them deep thought and as you design your tasks and projects use them as a way to create self-discipline in your life.

Is it easy? Absolutely not. But using this as a reframing tool. It gives you the ability to see things in a much more positive light. View your constraints with new eyes. View them as helping you not holding you back.

Chapter 15. CBT

According to Wikipedia, Cognitive Behavioral Therapy or CBT is a psycho-social invention widely used and backed by science to improve mental health.

It uses empirical research in the development of coping strategies to solve problems such as self limiting thoughts, belief, and attitudes.

Originally used to treat depression it has now been adopted by other health care practitioners and coaches for a myriad of conditions from anxiety all the way to lack of confidence.

It is a problem focused and action-oriented type of therapy. Perfect for someone looking to become more self disciplined in their life.

Windy Dryden is an influential thinker in the field of CBT. He uses this skill for coaching clients and in an interview with Alice Stapleton laid out the five components of self-discipline that need to be managed if we are able to adopt new habits leading to greater self-discipline.

1. Improvement. There has to be a desire for improvement and to set very specific goals that are important to us and we have to own them. They can't be cookie cutter type goals either. Your goals will not be mine and vice versa. If not, then we will not commit to them for long. This is especially true in the areas of nutrition and fitness.

2. Long-Term Self. Another way of saying take the long view. The changes will not happen over night. It takes time and sometimes it can be hard to see the end, if there is in fact an end. Some goals are lifestyle changes that will not yield a tangible result per se. It is important to list the benefits you are receiving and when you need to review them for motivation you pull them out and read.

3. Short-Term Self. According to Windy this is the area where people run into the most problems because the short term self is a pleasure seeker. It wants the easy way and does not want to face problems that can be faced tomorrow. This is part of us that wants to stay in bed even though we should go to the gym or wants to eat cake because it tastes amazing.

4. Executive Self/Mediator. This part serves as the mediator between our long and short selves. It balances between the two and is a very important component of developing self-discipline

5. Obstacles. The obstacles will be there no matter what. It is our attitude towards them that is going to determine our success at achieving a self-

disciplined life. Have a plan in place that you can refer to when the inevitable roadblock shows up.

Keeping all of these aspects of our personality in mind we need to realize that there will be times when we relapse and fall back into old patterns. That is OK and will be part of the process of change. Also, our beliefs of what is possible are what are holding us back. There is never a right time to start something but when we get stuck in thought patterns that want you to put things off until a future date it will never happen. By reframing what you have to do as something you want to do rather than something you have to do you are more likely to do it.

Do this next time, change a word when you have a task to complete, especially one you do not want to do. Say, 'I get to do X task.' Don't say, 'I have to do it.'

See the difference? By reframing the situation you are able to begin the task in a much better frame of mind.

This is also a way to trick yourself into action. Taking action is so important to getting things done. When you do not feel like doing something just start, much like we wrote in 'Just do something chapter'. It is imperative to developing self discipline.

Also, putting yourself in situations that are uncomfortable such as resisting the urge to smoke or overeat can be viewed as opportunities to develop self discipline and can strengthen your resolve. By going through the process you will find things that help you where you would not have found them if you had not started.

See yourself as someone that finishes tasks and accomplishes goals then take action. Consider it deliberate practice.

Chapter 16. First Principles Thinking

What is first principles thinking and how do we apply it to developing self-discipline in our lives?

According to James Clear of jamesclear.com, first principles thinking is the basic assumption that cannot be deduced any further.

An example would be when Elon Musk wanted to explore going into space exploration. He needed to buy rocket. Now for you and I this may seem crazy. However, Elon Musk knows something that we don't, and that is you can figure out anything if you can break it down into its component parts.

When Elon Musk spoke with people about purchasing a rocket to send mankind into space through his new company Space X he was told the cost would be about $65 million.

Usually that would be enough to stop someone in their tracks.

Not him, though, what he did instead was ask about the parts that made up a rocket.In other words, what were the materials and how much did each material cost.

He was told it was copper, metal, lithium, and a whole host of other materials that went into building a rocket.

He then calculated that the material cost alone in making a rocket was approximately 2% of the final cost in this case of $65 million. He said we can build a cheaper so he ended up creating his own company that he could control the costs going forward.

Whether or not that is panned out or not is not important what is important is the type of thinking employed and I want you to do that to your own life.

What is stopping you from attaining the goals you set for yourself?

What is stopping you from seeing other options that you could employ to move your life forward?

Let's say you want to start a business. Instead of

looking at the whole picture. Break it down into its component parts and understand that it is something that can be done.

For example let's say you want to open a convenience store what you would do and this is a very simple example, but what you would do is one find a location. Once you found your location. You would then apply for a business license. Once you obtain the business license, you would then have to purchase fixtures for the store, assuming it was entirely empty.

All the while you are doing this you are taking into account the costs involved and how much you will need to come up with. You would do this for every aspect of the store.

Instead of being overwhelmed. You break it down into manageable chunks that allows you to focus on one small thing at a time so that you can see the impossible become very possible.

I have referred to the book. The checklist manifesto more than once in this book. There's a good reason for that. What he is advocating works.

You can use this to develop self=discipline to move forward because now you are not wrapped up in analysis paralysis.

You are simply looking at the ways in which you can accomplish the small steps necessary to move your project forward.

I believe one of the biggest problems we face in our quest to better ourselves is the need to think we have to have it all figured out beforehand. That is simply not the case. The fact of the matter is this, break the problem down into its smallest possible chunks and then go to work on just one small aspect of the problem. Before long, I assure you the problems will be seen in an entirely different light. You will instead see the end result come about as a matter of course because you have taken the necessary steps in a logical sequence.

Elon Musk has been doing it this way for years and he is making the seemingly impossible seem, well, possible.

I don't believe Elon Musk has a magic secret. I believe he has figured out what works for him. It so happens to be something I believe can work for anyone. Get out of your own way and let First Principles thinking be your first course of thought as you approach a problem be it studying for an exam all the way to starting an international business. It can be done and you can absolutely do it.

Summary

So what have we learned?

In this summary. I want to go over nearly everything we studied in this e-book.

I realize there are a lot of theoretical ideas being posed here and what we want to do is break them down into a workable system that you can apply immediately to your life.

If I were to begin, in reality this is how I do it, I would begin with the foundational habits.

I think these habits should be the cornerstone of anyone looking to develop greater self-discipline.

By looking at your sleep and taking it seriously that in and of itself will lead you to better discipline almost instantaneously.

Why is that? When you are rested you make better decisions and it leads over into everything that you do.

When Bill Clinton was the president of the United States. He said that when he made mistakes, they happened when he was very tired. He is also famous for stating that he requires very little sleep and it would be difficult to argue that he was not productive.

I do not want to make this a discussion about politics and whether you approved or disapproved of his policies. It is simply to point out that when he made some of the choices that he made by his own admission he stated some of those choices were made when he was lacking in rest.

Apply this to your own life and make it a habit to get enough rest, your decision-making will be much more sound.

The next habit we've talked about at length is nutrition and like I said, I believe intermittent fasting is a viable option for you if you have struggled with your weight in the past. This is something for you to consider. You can possibly maintain a healthy weight by eating one last meal a day and then finding that you do not even miss it.

Of course, no matter what diet you choose to follow. Be sure to use good judgment in the types of foods that you choose to eat. Something else that I did not mention in the nutrition habit portion of the foundation chapter was this:

everyone is different. Everyone's metabolism runs a little differently within a range. Some people will be better able to metabolize carbohydrates, while others seem to run better on higher fat. It is up to you to determine which one you are if you are a person that seems to run better on fat.

Do what you can to avoid taking in excess carbohydrates, especially ones that are considered simple carbohydrates such as cakes and doughnuts etc.. Use your nutrition as a way to develop greater self-discipline you will find that it is much easier if you turn this into a game.

Exercise is another cornerstone habit that will lead to better health as well as warding off mental issues such as depression and anxiety. You need to fit it in whenever and wherever you can.

I am not going to tell you what type of exercise you should do. However, I believe some kind of stretching, cardio and strength or weight-bearing exercise is a good all-around approach to becoming a more healthy and centered individual.

The last habit we spoke about was that of mindfulness. You can also call it meditation. Recent advances in the field of psychology have discovered what Buddhist monks and yogis in India have known for centuries. A quiet mind centered on and in control of its own thoughts leads to greater productivity for avid practitioners.

It really does not take a lot of time either. By making it a part of your daily routine like we discussed in the morning ritual chapter you will see that you become calm and better able to handle stress because you are not allowing your thoughts to run away from you in 10 different directions. I like how Tom Sterner in the practicing mind puts it. When your thoughts are in control of you. They are like horses on a chariot without reins and you will go in circles. When you are in control of your thoughts and you have the reins in hand. The horses will do your bidding. You will become a much more centered and calm individual.

As you begin these foundational transformational habits, leading to greater self-discipline in your life utilize temptation bundling. When we spoke about it in the temptation bundling chapter the research shows that it works. By using something that you like, or is fun for you, such as watching a favorite show and combining it with something that you need to do on a regular basis such as exercising at the gym. It will lead to profound changes in your life. Be creative about how you want to go about this. I cannot stress it enough. This is so important to start with small changes and coupled them with things you enjoy doing. You can become a very focused individual. It is like the horses on the chariot you are in control of them.

At the same time, that you are using temptation bundling. So remember to do your best to wean yourself off of what I call empty time killers such as games on your phone. Mindless entertainment.

That's not coupled to a new habit they are trying to develop, endless music on your phone when you could be listening to audiobooks that are helping you learn something new. All of these things, you have got to get control of. When you do you will number one appreciate the times when you do get to use the mindless, easy distractions, coupled with your new habits.

You will get a better feeling from them because it is now a treat and there is no guilt associated with enjoying it because you are also accomplishing a goal such as exercise or cleaning the house or a myriad of other activities that are important but not time sensitive.

When you are starting something new, for example, you are trying to learn a new skill. What can happen is you will wait for the right time for that to happen. For example, if you want to become a writer. You may only write when you feel motivated to write, but as I wrote in the chapter -just do something already. I really worked to dispel that notion. You are going to have also. Just do something. In the case of writing just write one sentence and that's it, do not hold yourself to anything more than that, I can guarantee almost that as you progress, you will write more if that is the skill you're trying to develop.

Of course, it can apply to any skill that you want to develop. If you want to become a computer programmer, it will have to do with putting in the time learning how to code, and on and on. Depending upon the skill. I cannot stress enough the importance of just doing something. Getting words on the paper, getting the codes programmed on the computer, sewing clothes on a sewing machine because you want to make something for someone, etc. Just do something, even if you do not feel like and as you do this, something magical, almost happens.

You will find your purpose. As we spoke about in that chapter. Finding your purpose in doing it to the best of your ability will make habit formation self-discipline so much easier. When you find your true purpose that one thing that you want to do. Self-discipline will become second nature.

Just don't do it all at once. Look for incremental gains in everything you do. By applying 1% improvement each and every task you desire to get good at you find your purpose and you have the foundation in place.

All of these things will work together and you will become a juggernaut of productivity almost but not quite as if by chance.

I hope this book is able to get you onto the right

path for you is a lot of theory, but there's also a lot of practicality by applying what you've learned and incrementally improving on the foundations and on your true purpose. You are well on your way to accomplishing those life goals that you set for yourself.

I look forward to hearing from you and how you were able to apply the concepts of this book to your own life.

I hope you have enjoyed this book and found it practical and useful as well.

I encourage you to read my other books: **I Am An Empath**, which explores the gifts and vulnerabilities of people who are highly in tune, empathetic, to the wants and needs of others; and **I Am An Introvert**, which explains the unique advantages and disadvantages of being a person who finds and recharges their energy from within, as well as the four major types of introversion and what each of them means in terms of societal interaction as well as personal and/or professional growth development.

If you are looking for more information about Emotional Intelligence, I urge you to read the book I co-authored with Helen Glasgow, **The Emotional Intelligence Spectrum**.

Finally, please download a free copy of our latest book, **The Growth Mindset**, and its accompanying workbook, Growth Games, for a thorough exploration and practical implementation of personal and professional growth development.

Yours,

Joshua Moore

FREE DOWNLOAD

INSIGHTFUL GROWTH STRATEGIES FOR YOUR PERSONAL AND PROFESSIONAL SUCCESS!

amazon kindle   nook   kobo   iBooks

Windows   ANDROID   BlackBerry

Sign up here to get a free copy of The Growth Mindset book and more:

www.frenchnumber.net/growth

You may also like...

I AM AN EMPATH

ENERGY HEALING GUIDE FOR EMPATHIC AND HIGHLY SENSITIVE PEOPLE

BY JOSHUA MOORE

Am an Empath is an empathy guide on managing emotional anxiety, coping with being over emotional and using intuition to benefit from this sensitivity in your everyday life – the problems highly sensitive people normally face.

Through recongnizing how to control emotions you have the potential to make the most of being in tune with your emotions and understanding the feelings of people around you.

Begin your journey to a fulfilling life of awareness and support today!

You may also like...

MAKE ROOM FOR MINIMALISM

A PRACTICAL GUIDE TO SIMPLE AND SUSTAINABLE LIVING

BY JOSHUA MOORE

Make Room for Minimalism is a clear cut yet powerful, step-by-step introduction to minimalism, a sustainable lifestyle that will enable you to finally clear away all the physical, mental and spiritual clutter that fills many of our current stress filled lives. Minimalism will help you redefine what is truly meaningful in your life.

Eager to experience the world of minimalism?

Add a single copy of **Make Room for Minimalism** to your library now, and start counting the books you will no longer need!

FN№

Presented by French Number Publishing

French Number Publishing is an independent publishing house headquartered in Paris, France with offices in North America, Europe, and Asia.

FN№ is committed to connect the most promising writers to readers from all around the world. Together we aim to explore the most challenging issues on a large variety of topics that are of interest to the modern society.

FN№

All rights Reserved. No part of this publication or the information in it may be quoted from or reproduced in any form by means such as printing, scanning, photocopying or otherwise without prior written permission of the copyright holder.

Disclaimer and Terms of Use: Effort has been made to ensure that the information in this book is accurate and complete, however, the author and the publisher do not warrant the accuracy of the information, text and graphics contained within the book due to the rapidly changing nature of science, research, known and unknown facts and internet. The Author and the publisher do not hold any responsibility for errors, omissions or contrary interpretation of the subject matter herein. This book is presented solely for motivational and informational purposes only.

www.ingramcontent.com/pod-product-compliance
Lightning Source LLC
Chambersburg PA
CBHW070131260726
48658CB00001B/357